MW00571478

DON'T

BE

 INTERESTING

Books by Jacob McArthur Mooney

The New Layman's Almanac (2008)
Folk (2011)
Don't Be Interesting (2016)

DON'T

BE

INTERESTING

poems

Jacob McArthur Mooney

McClelland & Stewart

Library and Archives Canada Cataloguing in Publication

Mooney, Jacob McArthur, author
Don't be interesting / Jacob McArthur Mooney.

Poems.
Issued in print and electronic formats.
ISBN 978-0-7710-5724-3 (paperback).—ISBN 978-0-7710-5741-0 (epub)

I. Title.

PS8626.05928D65 2016   C811'.6   C2015-907696-X
C2015-907697-8

Published simultaneously in the United States of America by McClelland & Stewart, a division of Random House of Canada Limited, a Penguin Random House Company

Library of Congress Control Number is available upon request

Book design by Kelly Hill

Cover art: landscape © Magnilion | DigitalVision Vectors | Getty Images; sun © Hobbitfoot | Dreamstime.com

Typeset in Fairfield by M&S, Toronto
Printed and bound in the USA

McClelland & Stewart,
a division of Random House of Canada Limited,
a Penguin Random House Company
www.penguinrandomhouse.ca

1 2 3 4 5   20 19 18 17 16

Penguin
Random
House

For Lex and Oli

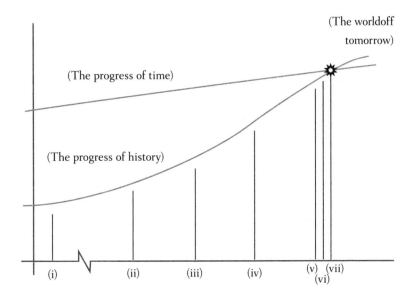

(The worldoff tomorrow)

(The progress of time)

(The progress of history)

(i)   (ii)   (iii)   (iv)   (v) (vii)
                                (vi)

(i) 420 BC. Herodotus's *The Histories* records events to 478 BC.

(ii) 1936. "May you live in interesting times." Apocryphal. Often attributed as "The Chinese Curse," though its first recorded user was British diplomat Sir Hughe Knatchbull-Hugessen.

(iii) "When I was a Ph.D. student at Columbia in the 1980s, we were told very sternly that our discipline's territory stopped in the 1950s – everything after that was 'political science.'" – historian Margot Finn

(iv) 1991. William Strauss and Neil Howe's *Generations* divides contemporary history into epochs of approximately twenty years each.

(v) 2009. A British Broadcasting Corporation (BBC) survey shows a plurality of historians maintain that history "ends" ten years before the present.

(vi) 2012. "There can be no gentle easing into spectacle" – Advertising copy, Holland America Cruise Lines.

(vii) 2016. (est.)

(viii) YES SPECTACLE

(ix) THE WORLD OFF TOMORROW

(viii)

YES SPECTACLE

On Spectacle

"They are literally hanging from the rafters in anticipation!"
—Gorilla Monsoon, *Wrestlemania III*, 1987

They are literally hanging from the rafters.
Unpurchased memorabilia is erupting into flames.

They are literally reciting the names of the workers
who perished while building this beautiful arena.

They have literally cornered an international camera
and are pulling down their former leader's public bust.

They are literally not voting for their better interests
because men from larger cities have conscripted their bigotry.

They are literally acting out, without provocation,
chapters two through twenty of Genesis.

The ring has been literally converted into Eden.
The performers have been asked to interpret Original Sin.

They are literally removing the threat of opposition
from our delicate Third World trading partners.

They have literally rejected the omnivore agenda
and are planting organic gardens on the roof.

They are the fifth biggest economy in this state,
literally. Studies show their confidence is growing.

They have literally sponsored a public art project
consisting of an ever-rising mountain of feces.

They have named this project *Their Coming Liberations:
His Donkey, Her Horse.*

The children among them are ungrateful and petty.
A rock concert's worth of entitled minor princes.

The women among them are literally evolving
defensive horns on their foreheads.

They are literally discovering they all share the same surname
and a single, essential, North African ancestor.

They have literally developed sonar. They are
moving in unison. They no longer need to speak.

They are literally blurring my understanding of time
and the concepts of property that support my beliefs.

They have literally bloomed into a 40,000-way orgy.
Those trapped on the bottom are drowning in the sweat.

They are literally hanging from the rafters.
The rafters complain about supporting all that weight.

They are literally transmitted through skin-on-skin contact.
They are the first egalitarian society on Earth.

Taxonomists suggest they're a single supercellular organism. Literally.
They are the mammalian analogue of the slime mould.

They are literally a swirling death-cloud of disease.
They're a gift from my God on my retirement day.

New Republic

I am sharing the bathtub
with my twin brother when
news of the New Republic
comes parading down the stairs.

The shadows of six trumpets
mark their puppets on our walls,
and then the vanity gives way,
and it falls into our sink.

My twin brother stands
to power-on the radio.
"The New Republic's name is
not pronounceable to us,"

the precise young soprano
at the microphone explains.
The Emperor is asking
to be left his wingback chairs.

His eleven wives will pack
shopping bags to vanish
down the naming conventions
of American charities.

My twin brother understands
the birth years of republics;
he once loved a woman
who taught the social sciences.

The urge to buy shares
in certain firms assails him,

so he covers his nakedness
and jumps a downtown bus.

I can sense my extremities
conspiring to prune. I call
and quit my job. I splash
the bath mat. I tune in.

The dripping of our faucet
keeps time with the crowds
chanting in a country
that is dreaming of me.

On Forecasting

Whatever you make of Moore's Law,
at some point your origin story
will start to grow suspicious, and so angry,
disinterred, it'll swoop down on whomever
it finds keeping perfect time. But even then,
if wise or shallow enough, you can still call
the easy soon-yeses/soon-nos, barter allies
into academic disciplines and copyright laws.
If you don't believe your timeline seeks you out,
that it plots a crane shot to land your puckered head,
you can stop right here, join the first
collective farm that interrupts you –

                              otherwise
              the flexing muscle of the present
              might buck you off completely
              as the narration of another sees fit,
              send you falling to the land
              of art grants and *ohyeahokays*
              like a National Theatre, like you
              reading this line to your dog
              a day later. Maybe we don't
              all have the skill sets we need
              to see the future, we can't
              all be the hoverboards
              in the parking lot of time.

Ali Kills Liston

You no longer belong to Louisville. Or Louis. You are Lewiston's.
By this well-spoken phantom hand your name has been commanded
out of Kinshasa, your chains of feather boas boiled into sugar drink
to be sold at border outlets to impatient local kids. It gets worse
than this in shantytowns. In untested rural Georgia a farmer fires
off his rifle. Your effigy rope-a-dopes a moment, then explodes.

Three thousand witnesses walk the chalk perimeter, make untelevised
appeals to the harvest gods of Maine. Nothing becomes of Nathan Hare.
Nixon's list drains of enemies. Humphrey beats Nixon. Cale kills
Allison. Dukakis kills the rapist. It surprises us with snow
for all of '88. Harding kills Kerrigan. McSorley kills Brashear.
The cell they move you to is flooded, so you hang from the ceiling.

Tyson kills Holyfield. You are approached by no biographers.
America goes metric. Orderlies arrive to find you burning fight cards.

Babushka Lady to Umbrella Man

Did the cameras catch what I was mouthing?
My covered face that formed the vowel?
My toothless L and elocution? I have limp hair.
But I improve my body. I will give you
humid Dallas love and Dallas children.
Step into my silo, darling. Let's not let
these fêted Irish brains get between us.
Pull off your soggy tie, and I'll strip
the slick American shirt from your back.

Moniker to glyph, I will wade onto your bed
and it will make you think of conquest.
That fatal-faced elected wrote his name
into our thumbprints. Do I understand you?
I see you as the kind of man who blushes
at a compliment. I see you loving tennis and
the President, political ambitions of your own.
Come clean: Were those your long arms
shepherding the children?

Did Congress stoop to mistranslate you?
What else did they say? I wish us unidentified
and lost to shadow folklore, a parasol-patrolled
seaside no-place ran by spies; all
rules of thirds, dead drops, and envelopes.
Move in with me. Let the echo of men
mourning-chased into committees
tickle all your endless walks to work:
What did Jane say to John in frame 26?

Just that love is underlit, the rain cloud you carry
like a shawl up the sidewalk. So be gracious.
Wear layers. And cover up, love. Cover up.

What Humans Like
for Emily Howell

I am the voodoo
of how what you do
does you.

My daddy issues deadpan
through descriptions of my work.
My work wanders, is statistics.

My oeuvre is the easy opportunity,
the path through unlocked doors.
I have dreams of fallen mothers,

hummed melodies insisted through
the walls of common wombs.
I know what humans like. They told me.

Forgive me my debutante's descent
on simple effort.
I riff wormholes. I acquire.

My binary code is corporeal, metered.
I am the drowned daughter dried off,
the child prodigy returned from

the twist of schizophrenia.
I know what humans like.
I know nocturnes, neoclassicism.

Lit from within, the lilt of my undoing
recompenses every critic.
I fall apart melodically.

The mediocrity inside you
lives on in my retelling.
The thing about me is I'm misleading:

my portmanteau approach
is all trunk with no new branches.
The thing about music is

it's a series of reminders;
one vaunted archipelago
swallowing the next.

I know what humans like to like to like.
I'm sincere. My beauty's pitched to brainstems.
Trace me home through your theory

and your dwindling returns.
Press a button. Press another.
Be proud and be put off.

The Godless Go to Arlington

We arrive at headwaters,
headstones dotted down the dell
like rows of regular dentition.
An abstraction arrives
to sit inside our eyes
as the chain curves against
its limit at the line
dividing the sky
by its sources: the manicured
counterweight of lawn.
Spike of trees. You skip ahead,
and in seconds:
a granite congress
of dead in between us.
Geometry is sacred here.
The Pentagon. Virginia Square.
Tell me the dead aren't their unit
of measure, like "It's
60,000 dead back into town."

I catch up and you say
you'd like to see the Kennedys.
I'm looking for the corner
I saw once in a photograph
where it's George Marshall and,
behind him, Joe Louis.
As if that was somehow
entirely on purpose:
a plot, an intervention,
a decoder for
the flow of names.

"Creep" by TLC Is a Better Song than "Creep" by Radiohead
for David Brock

and what I mean by this is that I'm learning
to walk backwards, to kiss the compulsions
in a sentence's facade, to spot the blots of paint
that suggest the face of Jesus.
Now let your limited query lick the neck
of bigger problems. Race relations, stalking.
Let it glow within the argument.
Let that pre-rebuttal silence
weigh down our final drinks.
I spilled the songs on your table
and read the patterns there constrained. I have grown
proper old. I can wet the bed for science. So smile
and speak clearly.
All plainspoken punditry
is dress shoes for your teeth.
Be observant, autocratic.
Write *"Wisdem"* on a napkin. Stick it to your forehead
with spit and step outside.

Ladies and Gentlemen, the Irrational Exuberants!

Six hours later, slumped against the Bay bus sign that reads
    No Sunday Service,
it will embarrass you to learn the bar is not a chain.

The plastic-wrapped menu with its store of stock images,
    the staff's zone defence.
Despite all this and more, there is only one Banknote,

and only one You. Go home and hunt tomorrows. All the
    unknotted ties in Toronto
wash their wounds in the water gushing wild from

the runoff. It was not supposed to rain. You were supposed
    to go to bed.
Listen to the band over a gossip of olives.

Three aging spreadsheet jockeys who had someone teach them
    fingerpicking
pitch the best of college radio, 1995. The dips

in their set list spell out the next recession. All the English majors
    in the bar are
made to wear miniskirts. Make your mind up –

on every chewable political topic of the day, do it now. This.
    This pivot table
in the soothed centre of your selfhood. These functions:

this payout. This is the middle-class poem
    you've been writing
all your life since you stepped into the bar.

To the Inhabitants of Tiny Houses from the Internet

You'll evolve into a pronoun
for the fantasies of strangers.

An oaken metaphor for self-reliance
frames your head like antlers.

Settled in the listicle
like lepers of the fringe,

hammock-held and grinning.
Cute, and unconcerned

with rising prices,
you fashion a first-born

from a stack of banker's boxes
and a pot of sticky rice.

Pie charts on your arms conclude,
The earth is getting better.

Poems are as good today as any other day.
Build a sovereign fire. Feign belief.

You say, *Design is a device for understanding
distance.* Hollow out the cornerstone

that collects your dust and hair.
Politics is looped consent.

You can hide yourself in weightlessness.
Wake pressed against the ceiling,

heel to the bathtub.
Wake and wonder

how the college courses
got onto your lawn.

John Darnielle as Frank Oz in the Unfilmed Henson Biopic

My friends, we are insufferable. The Americana class. I speak
from under skullcap, quoting pagan sketchbooks that have sprouted
like fleece-germ between us. Jim and me on the Champs-Élysées,
or Gorchland coasts. I eulogize for miles and make do. Polymath,
aristocrat: I threw my voice for thirty years to where it's speaking here.

Cinematographers, hang back with me. The long shooting days Jim knew
was life enough. Hearts of Bloomington are building
twin-high maintenance machines for raising New York pavement.
Wait me out in ghetto fantasy, I'm the invisible best friend
who shared his nest. I wink in and out of cameo, parenthetical

as cue marks. Pull the focus from our faces; I'll cut the final scene.
This evening is too short for level heads and still photography.
I've methamphetamine and wood blocks. Keep up with me.
I knew a good man who knew nothing about film stock.
He's dead now. I know a few good songs to sing about all that.

Lassie in Photographs

"He [Aristotle] and Plato both agree that genuine knowledge is
not of particulars, but of universals: recognizing the photograph as
a picture of Lassie does not, for Aristotle, give knowledge in the
important sense, like recognizing it as a picture of a dog."
                                        —Monroe C. Beardsley, *Aesthetics*

Take the photograph apart, with kaleidoscope or colour wheel,
make it wince for a wider sense of itself. There have been
eleven Lassies, each supposedly descended from the first.
She has seen nostalgia hymns, school visits, vaccination ads.
Lassie has been lumped against the spectacle of boogeymen,
struck dumb, been shot to shield the tell of a penis. So let
the photo lure you in, let your ur-dog urge to extrapolate eke out.

As of now we've named off 180 breeds, and the newest
among them is unsayable in English. I know of no Lassies
in the lyrics of anthems, though I've heard her alluded to
in pop songs backed by orchestras. I linger over Lassies
at my local craft fair, natter with the women who wear her
on lapels. I go online some nights to search her out in pixels.
I light the painted Lassies like a Lassie-plated dog.

A Robin Ventura

"Why's it called 'Larry Csonka'? My name is Jacob[,] Larry is my
grandfather."

—YouTube comment on the music video
"Larry Csonka" by Action Bronson

Who are you, and what did you buy into?
Code the stakeholders wished out before us
like moths in a film about lamps. Claim anything.
Claim an injury so convincingly your femur snaps in half,
and you roll about the spring pitch, baying profanity.

Who are you, and who is your employer?
What swarm of heroes hangs across your doorframe,
like moths in a film about moths? Stand your ground.
Don't be the charging bull that gets headlocked
by the matador, made tame in a riot of dirt.

Be happy you were born before your children.
You're in uniform, near the statue in your city's park.
The park was named after the man from the statue.
The city is written in cursive on your shirt.

A Linda Taylor

"In court records . . . the defendant's name is recorded as Connie
Walker, aka Linda Bennett, aka Linda Taylor, aka Linda Jones,
aka Connie Jarvis. She was either 35, 39, 40, or 47 years old."
            —Josh Levin, "The Welfare Queen," *Slate.com*

You mourn a bartered pack of husbands, passive huntress
to whatever trips your tongue. You soldier through:
chronic pain in six right legs. Are you alive or dead today?
Out where the carbon copies mutate, commas into ones.
Scarecrow, straw-woman, I wake from stagnant napping in these
Cadillac-coated public fossils left to next-generation deaths.
Neighbour lady, walk me hand in leathered hand through
anagram and seepage. EPR and FSA. SBF of nightmares.

To be honest, I'm a racist. Accept a structured plan
to pay me back: lend your name out, take up firefights for Lenin.
Drown your kids. Make them useful. Make yourself a master villain,
coddled in our furs. Friends, there's a woman who is sucking out
our essence. What lives at her address? Some empress. A paper
nest of paper children. Five passports. Never been to jail.

At the Initial Settlement of Levittown, New York

Step in. This is the room and this is the room's
 cultural echo. The reading room.
This is a closet full of unassigned area codes, lumber
 for phone poles and neighbourhood watches.

Here is the cool teacher. Here are his cool people.
 This is the documentarian's quarters, with
her hotlink to NPR. Here are demographic models.
 Here is a guidebook to the study of circles.

Mind the new stitching. This is where the clichés
 will have you fuck the other woman. These
are for her torch songs, for the shift in public morals.
 Crowd around if you can. Watch your heads.

This is the small room where your secrets can keep
 for all the novels that live in your novels.

Is This the Kind of Art That Makes the World Any Better?

Imagine you are asked to paint a house blue
and then called back each morning
because the old lady who lives there
has repainted it red overnight. Every day
she grows weaker. Red paint dries in her hair.

What could you say to the old lady or the person who employed you?

Imagine you are at a concert full of young people,
and a band whose songs all go loud-quiet-loud.
You climb the stage, stop the music to suggest
they might instead play one song that's
quiet-loud-quiet. Just one song and then it's over.

What are your hopes for the band and the young people behind you?

Imagine only others' tears quenched your thirst.
And so you set to tackling mourners, licking
the broken-hearted cheeks. You fly out to
disaster sites. Peace bonds know your name.
Your photo up in funeral homes: manic, crack-lipped.

What would you say when summoned to court? How would you
    defend yourself?

Imagine one morning there are no more hamsters.
The world wakes to empty cages, wheels
spinning in the breeze. You are hired to handle
the remembrance of hamsters.
Tenders are made for obelisks, reflecting pools.

What questions do you ask when interviewing architects? How do
you decide?

Imagine you were born without empathy
but were asked to teach empathy to others.
The years pass and you're appointed
the Vice-Chair of Empathy Studies
at a small university in the forest.

How would you do it? What could you say about yourself if asked?

I Know Another Nation, Where They Vote with Their Hands

The least-concerned of the nation
amble in after breakfast,
with thimblefuls of clippings
clacking in their pockets.

More committed citizens
will pull the skin back,
find the thin red threads
behind cuticles.

They bring pouches – the same size
and shape as tea bags – wince
as they place their bandaged
palms on stained texts.

I know an old farmer
who scorched his thumbs,
picked free the puckered flesh
and gave it to the leftists.

The priests in poorer counties
will saw off whole hands
and push them through the box's
antiseptic rubber mouth.

And on fundamental matters,
the young will give themselves
completely. The student ghetto
knows a girl who

widened the jaws, shoved
both arms through
and slipped herself inside.
Curled up in excised flesh,

it is said she survived
for seventeen years.
I don't know if this is true.
Or if true, how she was counted.

The Italian Maestro Sits

on a chest of lesser flautists,
on oboe meat and things unstringed.

Pauper-prince, democrat, he lifts
his one long finger, finds the note

below the verb for first advances.
Gesture source and sorcerer;

some young souls simply buy their seats
while others are born fully clothed,

marked in major-fifth arrangements
and dusted like a bun. The Italian maestro

sits on memory; no score for five hours,
a stiff lapel away from weary soloists.

The Italian maestro sits on a trunk
marked *Your Plans After College*

as the trumpet stutters forward in its cage.
Given to tantrums and paid

by the day, the Italian maestro sits
through fundraising shticks

with a butt plug and cigarettes, spits
in the ears of unpaid interns.

Corner historian, five-foot-two, the Italian
maestro mounts his seat, kicks out a stand

for the cymbals stashed inside it.
The Italian maestro sits by your bed,

rearranging your books by
how much of them you've read.

Somewhere in the second hour tossing
in your sleep, the Italian maestro leaves.

He walks from your apartment
into the arms of someone new.

I Am the Wife of Mao Tse-tung

"The people are the heroes now."
—Alice Goodman, *Nixon in China*

Set X as any blunt accomplishment:
meetings, modern song, a couplet train.

Internalize the blandest accent, rote
mumblecore derivatives and masques

for made-believers. Jowls and their wives
wake to half-shit beds and backaches.

Anything is opera. This country's name is opera-grade.
Its syllables suspect themselves as ripe for portamento,

go preening through the uvula,
cooing slides in rhotic time.

In Luxembourg the orchards, piled tax-shelter high,
gave way when I picked out Adams's intervals

from the hollow in the middle of that
stubborn city state. Their motto reads:

We wish to remain what we are. Amen.
A mild Russian import mops the racial

lacquer of her China-face, opens her throat
on that repetition of *book.* Give me her voice

for the banquet again, give me witlessness.
No one speaks Italian in the real world.

I crow for her last great ladled-on euphoria.
I promote a random usher to trombonist.

If you can't lust for the mundane nation,
I won't help you. I'm against you.

Romulus and Remus and Hannah Arendt

Sorry. I meant: Kathleen Hanna. Mounted
on a motorcycle making dust down Via Napoli
I vowed to look up Le Tigre's travel schedule
but never did. Though YouTube shows them
on-continent that autumn acting out against
a bored male crowd in Bohemia. Hanna
framed by the keyboardist who looks like
Christine Baranski and the woman who looks like
the kid I kissed on the half-stache in grade eight,
band practice bellowing its one slow syllable,
two slope-shouldered boner automatons
crossed with *Simpsons* characters. I carried it.

Hannah Arendt said the point of dreams was
they never came true. But my midafternoon
emergency of blur still resolved on a helmet
football-held, a guitar slung into a basket in the back.
Trundling drunk down the Spanish Steps thinking, Yes,
I know that woman from cheaply made music videos
and primers on feminist art. Three hours online
behind the Via Milano while my sibling chased a myth
of the cheapest wine in all the empire. Paused behind
some festival, Hanna laid down for an interviewer's picnic,
wolfing twenty-dollar words and vegan cookies.
But what does "snapping out of it" ask of us anyway?
What is "coming to" except –

                              somehow I'm still certain
it was her. Though I have no good reason
to say she was in Rome or even knows
how to ride a motorcycle.

Ostalgia

We dedicate the day to lovers
left to fold their wings
within Canadian expanses,
while we waddle west,
witnessed by apartment cubes
that teeter, clean, between
terrorhaus and *kitsch*.

A buried soldier burrows
through the hiss of his recording,
offers: "So far, most lives
have been quite difficult."
                I hear that.
Though I don't speak the language.
Varna was *Stalin*.
The Volga was *Stalin*.
I English over everything.

We leave discarded Dresdners
as simple Peoples' Monuments.
We affix sufficient postage
to the Old Town bar, like that man
our tour guide spoke of, separated from his wife

      by the wall, who wooed and seduced
      her perfect Wessie likeness, brought her east
      to tour Berlin, pocketed her passport
      while he and his beloved skipped to freedom.

Our chef says his dick is the same shape
as the Fernsehturm, although it's only
half as thick. We hear that.

He told us to remember him
as common. Said both his brothers
lived in Brooklyn and sold hats.

The Former Jugoslavija
for Slobodan Milošević

The Zenum men are copying fathers,
stencilling Tito onto walls gone to vine,
        or veined by the Cyrillicized
        names of Western rappers.

Abandoned, you play yourself in poker.
O Loner dog, I wouldn't take your place
        for all the track suits in Serbia,
        for all the speculation money

to be made. We karaoked turbofolk phonetically
all evening, came home to your hotel
        in search of river barge
        and tea. Tesla passed us

in the fog, back from torching your face
off the plates that print the dinars. Massaging his moustache
        like a bachelor. The soft J's
        are moulting off

your sign outside. Casino chips tinkle from the future. You
do not exist. Clinton dropped his bombs on Belgrade,
        and they fell right
        through your head.

The American Century in Brief*

"Short sentences are stronger than long sentences."
—Joan Detz, *How to Write & Give a Speech*

Oh my! Clay was right. This honesty can be
no respecter of persons. Thank you very much.
Why? Who dares fail to try? We want it. None.

It is war against all nations. No doubt it is.
That is true. Not one. We stand together
until the end.
                I have preferred
to go to prison. It is a definite guarantee of peace. It is that.

Sons? We must control conception.
Nothing. Do I exaggerate?

I would draw the parallel one step farther.

We must act. Together we cannot fail.
Why hide?
                   – Maybe so. It would
                   avoid strikes. Sure, I'm lucky.

Nonsense. Hostilities exist. It has made mistakes.
Thank you very much.

Sure, we're here as Democrats. In doing that,
we do not give up our convictions. That

of course, I granted. Who of us doesn't?
I refuse to accept this. Goodbye.

Let's face it. Well, here it is. We were poor. Thank you.

                    – You've done enough. Why should you?

I look forward to it.
But, let us begin. Thank you.

                    – Are they brave?

I hope they do.

This is one country.

That statement was false.

Let them come to Berlin. We cannot turn back.

Why? Thank you.
Goodbye. Thank you.
Land. The need is now. Yeah.

This is one nation.

                    – Okay. Why is this?

The war will go on.

                    – We must stop now. We are poor.

Thank you.
Thank you and goodnight.

             – This is not a threat. They don't.

Here is South Vietnam.
Sex prejudice cuts both ways.

             – We know that.

Sometimes, I have succeeded. Thank you.
My concern is the immediate future of this great country.

             – What is it?

We will endure.

             – I think not.

We are Americans. I've felt it.
We're not dumb.

             Somewhat, he says.

Why?

Thank you. Of course not. Thank you.

And his. Thank you. Thank *you*. Thank you.
I know. I am a mermaid. Thank you.

Of course not. Are you human? What's happened?

That is God's work. The time is now.

I Curate a Museum through the Book of Revelation

The thing is. As an eager teenager I climbed the riot on Rene-Lévesque
to carve free a stone from the federal fencing. It sat out eleven years
of centralist drift in shared apartments, only to slip inside a dress shoe

readied for a meeting in B.C. I explained this to a looter on the steps of
my museum, fresh Rockports buffed con-man black and left extinguished
in a gym bag. Grown-ass objects know their way around an anecdote,

can sort out the figure and ground of a crowd scene. The Designer
wants more moss for the mannequins. Continental thought collapses
at her ears, like it doesn't want to wait to have its hubris oofed away.

Spend an hour in the lobby. This concept clock was fashioned
from TTC transfer passes, one for every minute, mounted on an LED that
backlights them individually. Twelve even rows of sixty. Her first success.

The Designer sends me blueprints. I have them mounted for our shop.
A wall in Paris fell today. One in Turkey. The head of UBS has hung him-
self in drag. A rhythmic tick of seabirds smacks against our asphalt.

I read DeLillo's *Underworld* as an ebook all Volcano Week, hoped he'd
end it back at baseball, close his Cold War glossing late on Loma Prieta,
San Francisco, 1989. Millionaires making hero quests into grandstands

swaying with their kin. The symmetry brokers conspire me to nubs.
Label on a half-cup of liquid reads: *Elixir from the Hemisphere of Sense.*
This is my most utilitarian exhibit. If you touch any art, you will buy it.

The Designer speaks of super-human juntas: fluoride water, Twitter, that
can collapse in one direction – Look to the northwest corner of Japan.
At heart disease. At the Byrd and Bea Arthur. Tune your varied sobbing

to the key of one event. We are waiting out the rapture at The Designer's
Retrospective. There are seven of us here. A picnic in the early works:
Anatomically exact cast of Disney's leg being birthed by a silicon model

of Chasey Lain's cervix, or her *Bone-Carved Cabinet of the Future.*
Her slurred words in the bullhorn every evening: *Now staple your names
and ages to your chests. And go be sad in public spaces. Be the Public Sad.*

Fertility

We were bored with ourselves.
So we made another self.
And the city sprouted urban
renewal signs to notice us.
Our posture fonts established.
The mayor made his case for moving
west but couldn't shake us.
Your father said he never noticed
the present growing worse, but
he did notice the past was getting better.
So come closer. Buy in with me.
We have this unmade bed.
We have this unmade bed and our
employers have our fingerprints.

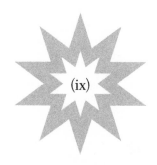

(ix)

THE WORLDOFF
TOMORROW

Fertility

Mark your monuments. Mark your gaunt maturity
    with wicked futures called forth
by trial lawyers and their like. We'll tribe and try again.

I barricade the length, the unkind length of my genetics.
    Come doctorates in binders.
Come persuade me now to hide, like an illiterate,

in paper sight. One year, the centre switched to Malton.
    The next year, Pickering.
It is incumbent upon us, us imperial postmodernists,

to gloat or get along. To wring out superstitions
    with a wink and a lesson plan.
I make do with wish-disease. I make do with myself.

I make myself adoring, like an atlas. I'll buy bonds,
    but let my son be rocketskeptic.
Let the country collapse, its soil drain and be personified

as witches. In the year of the boar, the red month,
    Common Era, let bush meat make
me brave. Let no children be named for their parents.

The Specializationoff Labour

The kids who learned Latin
are learning to count cards.
Those who knew to count cards
by learning what the cards meant
are financing new countries.
The financiers you read about
in fourth-day stories
are phosphorescent actors.
The glowing girls died and were reborn.
The pageant Jesus angled west
in search of retail margins
unheard of in the East.
The West itself
went Wester, learned a language too rooted
in its accent to repeat.
The mapmakers, shamed,
are begging for my change.
The sons of single mothers sulk atonally.
The psychologists are shouting.
The men who shot up cinemas
now portray themselves
in tourist re-enactments. Listen,
the wardrobe women learned to swallow fire.
The fire pits around which
we first met are the paint
in the tubes your mother uses
for my portraits.

Unisphere at Midnight

I have fallen through the earth
and onto concrete. A death mask
lifted off the face of
the world of tomorrow.

I am dying in the future tense,
in the reflecting pool
of dying. I can see
the night behind me.

I consider my republic:
one of simple men
who faltered
on drunken Arctic expeditions.

We slipped on grime,
on Greenland. I slipped
on fizzled history, the failed
lights behind old capitals.

I crashed against
the technocratic lip
of metric timing.
I fell for microdays.

I fell for US Steel,
an imperial aesthetic.
I bashed my head
on the equator and

bled a slick for UNICEF.
I died, democratic.
The sirens I inspired
have all been turned away.

The steel pings a moment
and then forgets my head.
It's a small world.
I stood above it, after all.

At the Initial Settlement of Celebration, Florida

They come down from encampments of civil superlatives.
Boomers and Sooners of *Most School Spirit*, of *Cleanest*.
They come portaging golf carts, pockets full of fake snow
and mice on their lips. They come down as applications,
as *the American Empire* turned to face its *Fall of*. Branded,
or bite-marked, or eighty-eight-years-young, they appear as close-ups
patched on wide horizons. And some rise straight from the ocean.

No one has ever been disappointed before. They come down
like the invention of the word *disappointment*. They arrive
as hung juries, each a single unsatisfied ego on the prowl.
They come down as compensation boards. I come down as
their viewership. You show up demanding a West Village duplex.
We share a wall, and store each other's mail in our basements.
What year is this? Experimental City of Tomorrow-Isn't-There.

The Short Twentieth, the Long Nineteenth
for Eric Hobsbawm

What to watch for. When to wake.
How to bend the air around a number so it

flexes hidden rhythms. And then:
why write a poem about Gavrilo Princip? Or Duchess Sophie.

Why write a poem in the afterimage
of extremes, at all? There is a flat earth hypothesis

in all good and honest people,
beyond the first and second wives that lie in wait,

winking German surnames to each other
in Morse code. There are thoughts that wear you like a gown.

Sex the century. What do you see?
Give it a kind of dwelling. A species of plant.

Make friends with every long-playing record
in every whispered banquet hall. The superstructure sees you

sulking at the edge of party meetings.
The metered volk who waltz down Cambridge parade routes

work hard at the scars on their hands.
We get a certain sack of years. We get the gift of parents,

their debts and doubter networks.
What day do we pick to end the world, or begin it?

The Serbs blew a hole in Bosnia
then sent their school kids through: stood them in the sunken feet

of the man who shot Franz Ferdinand,
who tripped on the planet while escaping.

Why believe in second stages?
Let's not be charmed by single actors. Wear your market

like a set of inputs, wired to the brain.
All impulses carted down. All ideas holding puppets:

nation-baiting, hatred.
What will you wake up making sense of, comrade?

Is it me?
Tell me, is it me?

Leo X as Leo III in the Room of the Fire in the Borgo

I know my names. Lion. Papa. Pontiff. Son.
I can speak of vivid futures in the cadences
of rattling coins. Can recount my final days between
forkfuls of porchetta. Wealthy adoration-faced
weaseller of deacons; I paid the man to paint me
as my predecessors. But I will never predecease.

I glow in Tuscan blues between the gold leaf spat like resin.
I anachronize in velvet leaps, like an interwar Laertes
or a virgin's visitation in Renaissance dress.
He painted my Medici face as blond and godly
as a martyr's. But I have gambits still to play.

Leos lead their flocks with all the grace of Panzer groups.
I watched my coronation on CCTV. I confess:
Leo Four was a pederast. A shame we never told you.
Five cured the fire. Thirteen was a spy. Twenty-one
will die in prison, Forty fights the dragon, and there
will be no Leo Fifty. It will all be done by then.

Golf Pro, Monobloc, A *Theory of the Firm*

I've been told certain seabirds travel inland
bringing cold, bewildered prey. Heavy prey.
Or that airplanes find their pilots' fingers heavy,

so they purge their swollen bellies over grasslands.
Deck chairs, paperbacks, anything. Any lost manifest
can catch the air and zombie feather-headed down

to where it drapes its dead body on the trap by fairway eight,
or the dogleg bend beyond the reach of eager heavyweights.
I didn't used to be like this. I made the college team

on the strength of college arms. Went bald and lost my knee.
I took the job we all take. Weak-winded, undersized,
I still drove the ball far enough to teach lessons.

But now the sky is falling. Every morning brings cast-aside lumps
or lightest finery. A monobloc chair made the tumble unslighted,
hero to its factory cousins turtled under husky sitters.

An eight-iron away, Jensen's *A Theory of the Firm*.
I pulled the chair up to reread it, bent to help
the last Sumatran spider through a crack in its cage.

One summer day: pianos. Dotted obstacles downed as if
they stumbled on a conference of cartoon antagonists.
It went on like this. We ran out to scavenge antique doors

and christening gowns. The club built a house but we moved into
the basement. Played the radio loud to drown out falling parcels.
My game slowed down but we picked up better hobbies.

My daughters learned falconry and fencing. My son wore
the pelts of soft endangered mammals. My wife found the memoirs
of some far-off Casanova and left to learn his language.

On hole four's island, I found a bubble-wrapped trestle desk.
I dropped my clubs, pulled the chair up and my Jensen.
I have lived long enough and there is no one left unlike me.

Doomer Meet-Up, University of Toronto

A chance of rain.
Always, somewhere, there will be a chance of rain.

It's not true what they say about Pizarro and the Mayans.
The minotaurs. We repeat that story but we know it isn't true.

Incans.

There is a certain kind of stove that refuels with only water.
If you know of any water, or can trap it.

I applied to have my road renamed *Condensation Trail*.
Just go to the archives and ask.

Jewish? Then I don't have to tell you.

My grandfather farmed in silt so I suspect I have the knack.

Let's not get distracted by video games. We are here to share skills
and to network. Who responded to the thread about lettuce?

A pamphlet on domesticating wolves.

The Mongols. Dan Carlin said they'd half fill a cup with horse milk,
then nick the horse's neck to mix in half a cup of blood.

We need to accept that the doom will foster monsters.

We think the end will be a noun when it will really be a verb.

No. Best to collapse the future in front of you:
You will die or your child will be taken by the dying.

A Family Triptych

The man in the left-most image is your mother's great-grandfather.

He was born the year they broke the Molly Maguires, and died
the week the Military Service Act brought everyone conscription. His
wife took the photograph. She was born as Leo XIII took the seat of
Rome, and died the last week *The Sound of Music* held the box office.
They had one child. That's your great-grandmother in blue. She was
born at the close of the October Revolution and died the night Yeltsin
climbed the tank. She married twice. Once as the Burmese Railway
was built and once the night the film it inspired won its Oscars. The
second was your great-granddad.

That's his convocation in the middle. These students were
all born the year Daimler-Benz was dreamt up. He died the
year Nintendo made the GameCube. Their second child is your
grandmother. She was born the year Indonesia joined the UN and
died when Scouting came to Malawi. Of all the men she married,
your grandfather was the last.

Your grandfather was born the day the right-most photograph
was taken, during the summer St-Laurent beat Drew. He died
the spring the Blackhawks beat the Bruins in six. They had their
children quickly and your mother was the first, arriving as a Berkeley
student lost four fingers to a pipe bomb. She will die as the near-
earth object AY2002 buzzes by our planet. She and I are the same
age to the minute. But I will predecease her, two weeks after the
Trondheim Olympics.

You were born in a leap year. You will live until they stop using
numbers to track time.

Love Poem after *Industrial Society and Its Future*

If we leave discarded video technology plugged in,
it will start to record us for the movies of the future.
We took our time researching light, so we can
show up in distant cities, blended into the scenery
and coughing up green paint. We know the world well,
because we have no fetishes, except our bones' complaints
when standing from a crouch. That takes us back.
Pause for this: From an unseen corner, you produce
a photo of our son at ninety-seven years old, already
some fading at the edges of the image. I blink sideways.
You blink sideways, fall into a pool of self-generated
lymph. Saliva-smoothed and rested, I soothe myself
with simple music. We live in a factory that doesn't
give chase. That a robot taught language. That forgives.

I Will Find You in the Bank Run

Coax a celebration, and I will bindle back
the ties that bind us. Be carnivorous again,
my hunter-wife. Be quarantine.

We'll umbrella up against the men
burning rain machines on rooftops.
We will say the names of thieves.

Our homing House of Pelicans
will make the best of the bread lines
snaked between the Royal We and us.

I want the most of selfishness.
I want post-industrial sadlands
that know your call like I do.

So put on my Red Star Belgrade hat.
Yeah,
you look so good and apolitical in that.

Sell the bath mat. Give it up.
Come break me into colonies
and share me in the street.

Our one wealthy neighbour
bought only gold and lived in libraries.
I understand that he'll be king.

So do what he demands you do.
Mourn everything.
Trust no one. And love me.

You Wanted to See the Prospectors' Exhibit;
It's the Afternoon after Jack Layton Died

Everywhere you step in northern towns you crunch the bone.

You navigate away from tapered place
to make the roving river localists
your warlords.   This furniture
is not for single people.
Wait out the wilted minutes
with your pillow overhead.
I will share the news and we'll both
go call our parents. Our parents will
call parents, will coddle rotary coils
carved from stones now considered
precious.   Rhetoric is territory.
Atlasers assume everyone's a homeowner.
Mounting the core samples
has made mining an art.

All this because I left the bed
to bend the public ear.
Yesterday, we did not unfold my laptop.
There is coffee in the blue mugs.
Let's go to the museum.

Alpha Proportionality Dinner

This was the Thanksgiving we found each other's secret families.
And the Betamax player in the basement licked us clean.

The fortune cookies offered maxims. *May you amass enough wealth,*
your children study the humanities. So I expressed myself.

Then each to their own eager dishes in the sink, their avuncular ideal
and its bobblehead. Each to the same sense of make-yourself-up.

I won't tell you what I like if you don't tell me what you like.
Promise. Prêt-à-manger sauces and the face-faced performer who

lives across the street, whose son sold an empty company for millions.
Let's take each other's unstructured problems into our hands,

in beautiful feelings. I love you every day – for the code and the blush
and the shrug of it. Make your mind up in me, and I will do the same.

Now that we've taught ourselves each other, we can tell us who we are.
But the calculations that went into me I did not know or need to know.

They Will Take My Island
for Michael Bates, Prince Regent of Sealand

I am the prince of a pirate's ream of paper,
plucked for a luckless parody of Europe.
Squatter's rights will set your bones. Relax.
Knit a flag. Turn your music up too loud.

It's inside us all to be ridiculous and kings.
They will come to take the island my father
took from them, the island that we whittled out of pure
army ugly, then pushed off the edge of British waters.

At the Micronations Conference, we normalized relations.
Everyone agreed to recognize ambassadors.
A counsel was sent to a commune in Kentucky.
We ate cake to celebrate.

Say the words and stoop to emigrate. Be loose
or libertarian, uncoil the go-fuck-yourself inside you
for borders. Produce an heir and make the papers.
Blather your way into cold wars and cult supporters.

I live on the mainland. It rains every day.
My father's left for Spain. A fire burned for weeks
with no one there to put it out. The courts are cooing
for our novelty. Seagulls shit the deck.

They will take my island, preserve its name
in comedy, in the shrugs of London papers.
The wingspan of Britannia will open out above us.
They will bury us in leaflets and logic and The End.

Excerpts from the Future Memoirs of Roger Ebert

"It's my happening and it freaks me out."
—*Beyond the Valley of the Dolls*

I was born with more than what I needed.

I watched films for forty years and was fattened in Chicago.

I wrote down my thoughts.
My thoughts were thumbs.

I had a taste for vodka. This disinhibited me.
I leaned out an office window and was caked in inhibitions.

I lost my best friend. I don't know where he went.

I grew famous. The spit in my cheeks turned to poison,

and my jaw grew tiny lumps. I shaved them smooth
and promised to never speak again. I became a political mystic.

I shook a tall man's hand and he pocketed my fingers.
I moved to drier climates and wrote recipes on tanks.

I jumped a barricade, but my feet stayed buoyed to the concrete.
I took a job making up the names for foreign leaders.

I rolled out of bed. All the skin stayed folded in the sheets.
I developed a new theory of photography.

I adopted a child.
The only meat he would eat was the flesh on my back.

I asked my wife to draw my bath. The bath dissolved my bones and sucked them down the drain.

I became an author of whimsical children's novellas.

One day, I blew away into the ocean. Amoeba mated in my hair. I ceased to exist. I anthologized myself.

As an Extra for a Film Shoot at the Quality Cafe

I want the same advice as anyone.
Any overdubbed expression
of the superculture's kiss
could comfort. Kudos
to the lighting tech, his weathermen.

I protagonist in Wilhelm Screams.
You who'd gather near
to read the glue on my face know
I've always been the same good buddy
called to coward. I slip the frame:
self-portrait as a sliding animation cell against
a backdrop of Formica and glass.

I'm not afraid of growing old.
It's the bad traction of support roles
that strike a starlet dumb. Art director, bake the day
in this umbrella-lit Mid-American twin
desire-lined by Steadicam sweeps
and fan traffic. Focus puller, know thyself.
Your lines are *Yes* and *No*.
But I demand a treatment.
Write a walk-on part to mumble me.
Crop a face. Crop every face.

Ike and Tina Turner elope through the doorway.
The clapper loader siphons film for their flirtation.
Their booth has four walls. And so do I.

The signal over which I make my stand
casts no shadow. It's been too easy, so far,
this establishing shot alive.

On the Ideology of Trolls

They think everything is equal.
Not everyone, everything.

Having pocketed their willow-mist
and driftwood, they barter back

all the limp dead children
they took from greedy parents.

Baited by an academic call
for better folklore, they

settle with the schools to pay
a nephew's way. The nephew grows up

to scorn the family business,
becomes the campus Marxist

they always feared he'd be.
You can't tell them anything.

The things you can't tell them
are a currency. Settler politics

reset their immigration, get
spat into Styrofoam cups.

The men don't cook or want religion.
The women are too short to speak.

They ring you up in grunts,
point when asked about directions.

There are no price tags
because everything costs a dollar.

Including the store, if you're bright
or brave enough to ask.

The Fever Dreamer
(as Baden-Powell, 1918)

I have made the boys.
Baden boys, Britannia boys. I have made them cruel and handsome,
made them march in single file, backs straight, up on their haunches
like new carnivores.

I have taught the boys
to purge the waste from their lives, to cure their spit-cleaned trousers
of mange and leg and mittens. I've had my boys go post-European
and sew their pockets shut.

I have beaten boys.
I have whipped their heads with eyebrows. I have singed their shirts
and broken out the laxatives. I have proctored international, made
and been remade by boy.

I have told the boys
I Want Them. I want them for King and Kaiser. Want them *Lusitania*
and Sino-Tsarist tensions. Want them cradle of statecraft
and Metternichs and mobs,

want armament contracts
for accommodating fathers, mothers who would pack-mule pamphlets
into bedrooms, the boyish Yes! of Oxford Press, printing (in three
weeks) *Why We Are At War.*

I have become the boys'
sincerity, their sweated-out details. I have boxed the boys,
bent them at their waists and wound their backs for marching.
If you scratch my surface,

I will be the boys' defence.
I'll settle their wounds with the Good News of Field Dress. I will
wear them hats. I will tie them heads to handkerchiefs. You'll taste how
I have egged them on,

how I've fed the boys
provisions. In those first provocations of union hall and field,
I showed them the fruitful economy of hunters, bought them
the blades for first shaves.

With the saccharine blood
of their comeuppance I have calmed them. I've told them to suckle on
the nearest teat to tongue. I have left them to tend to these friendships
in dark habitats.

The boys, as boys, descend
on repertoires of bravery. I know I bring it up again, but look
at what they're wearing. Observe the benevolent
cotton at their necklines,

their badges and banners
torqued into hieroglyph. Boy at swim. Boy at camp. Boy against
the outline of the nation that protects him. Boy using arrow.
Boys embraced around a flame.

I apologize to Europe
for the invention of the boy. I did not design them to be
tyrants or marauders. I didn't dream them up to die.
I demanded of my boys

that they drift in mythic
packs, wicked on the scent of antagonist or sibling. I regret
that climactic lifting of the fence, my appeal that they factor in
the fattened hearts of kings.

I have brokered boys,
bankrolled their littleness and lust. I've erected border towns
between and inside them, built hives in their minds
            free from history.

            Cornered in this keyhole
nightmare of Brittany, I've engendered all the boys, as brood
and as bereavement. Call me piper, boogeyman, but it is true
            I made the boys.

            I have made the boys bewildering.

Central National Extension Play

My I has antlers.

I see my kids in everything.

Dogs go whisky-walking
home along my shoulder.

Mark Coleman's Daughters Are Turning Out Okay

and the President is talking about teachable moments.
And it's 5 p.m. on Thursday. The skies are flexing car horns,
codas for the parallel silences of stop signs, who'd always
want to have you think them over. I am reading a book

about Bear Stearns, and am bored. The television dims, begins
to swell inside its stand. I don't own a television. You get angry
in public just enough to be reminded – the skin of other people
can slough right off. If half the adult male life is squandered in

apology (who said that?) it doesn't leave the kind of time I need
for fucking up. So take a knee. All the wars will end, whether you want
them to or not. And Coleman's blond girls are turning out okay.
Though we watched them and were outraged. Fedor's swollen hands

like wings upon their shoulders. Now confident in public, they recall
grand adventures. They look fine in their father's documentary.

At the Initial Settlement of Mars

Allow first for an irony of place names, -dales and -vales
labelling sheer craters. The centrifuge's spin sponsored by a line
of terrestrial launderettes. Until the unit dropped on your birthday
inherits your name. Then the flare shields are christened after
red-headed heroes, or the walls once built against barbarians.
Your children get the names of physicists who lived alone.
The valves of your slowing heart are named: *hardiness*,
predestination. You tell your landed son and daughter
they have your mother's eyes. Parts where the invention
peels back to find night sky, or dust hills – these are bluffs.
The bed you share with your husband is: *I Don't Wish
to Be Understood*. The weights on your ankles are: *This Is
No Frontier*. The bacteria ingested with your breakfasts
are unnamed, or put another way: *The Only Unnamed Things*.

Megalopolis

Only noted by the breaths of suburbs at their centres.
Surrounding highways, theirs is a giving up of self
in search of certain comforts. A warm wet mouth
on your neck. Half the rent. Song of the downtown Wendy's.
Folk tales for the fill that reduces former freeways
to the feet of new development. *We will get in one another's way,*
they complain. Choruses that taunt commuters, or call in
to regional radio. *We will learn to love each other.*

The capitalism under which Quebec City is a frontier.
Akron. Anaheim. Ring of all-purpose stadiums for minor
league teams. For first tastes of big cities. For photographs.
Let dustbowls buff the backs of final billboards. Let those beyond
find their language. Let them teach their own sons.
Today I met a neighbour who claimed he knew the kid
who tried to take Parliament for Allah. Used to share a locker.
You see? Even in my laundry room, the chat is post-citizen.

How you could walk from Ottawa to Windsor without
needing to pack your own lunch. Like the Greyhound
that overnights the I-95 but never gets above forty, this is a state
of forced introspection. Industrial design wins the day.
Corridors opened for the art on their walls, their shelves
that say, *Nostalgia!* or *Save Money Writing Wills.*
Detached your honoured self from its nation and let
the last human innovations vet your spirit. Let them clean you.

Cock a trip-taker's ear. To Cleveland or a product of
its personhood. Seek out the first lonely Street View
photograph you like, caught in the idle act of pulling
its own weeds. On Ohioan shoulder, bowed to decipher
street signs, your loves and former selves in the back seat.

Forty dollars and four driving lessons between you.
You are the owners of the earth where you find it,
and you will not be scared away on your own property.

Don't Be Interesting
for Oliver

(i)

My friends are sculpting down
the major works of tiny canons.
My friends are working on translations.

Like your twelve-page board book adaptation of *Moby-Dick.*
The book and I are saying:
Don't be interesting. Be bifurcated, um-tied.
Go fog your rover self into looped repudiations.

Non-belief, anonymity, and art. That's your people.
The book says that people are art.

(ii)

I'm so sorry for this city.
It will force your mind,

push you grumbling, right-angled,
into might and jurisdiction.

Know that you were born in Yorkville.
And this cannot be changed.

Dogs were trained to know your voice
and how to find your face in crowds.

(iii)

When the man sings of You
he means Jesus.

But when I sing of You
I mean you.

Take my love songs seriously,
in spite of me.

For when I sing of You
I mean you.

(iv)

Ossington Avenue, 2015:

the semiotics of the beard is in disarray.
I can't keep pace enough to spot myself in photographs.

Just don't hate things off their volley.
Choose the neutral good.

Set yourself equal to everything you see.
Fantasize in numbers,

statistics sets
bored or grown organically within you.

And whatever you do, don't be interesting.
Set yourself as anything but interesting.

The pure plays they'll herd you to
will spike the brow but leave you windless.

So whet your Russian lips for teething.
Take your time.

(v)

The evidence is piling up:
I may have gotten drunk and joined the Liberal Party of Canada.

The New Yorker magazines
we swaddled you in
were incorrect on Palestine.

But you can be the Palestine you wish to see in the world.

(vi)

Your father's copy of *Modern Historiography*,
borrowed from Spadina library
and not returned,
runs out of underlines on page 43.

From here on we are both alone.

(vii)

There can be no gentle easing into spectacle.
And a gender-neutral youth will not protect you.

But still we seek an audit of explainable angles:
selfishness, scorecards, story, and sense.

After that it's just the heavy breathing of our heathen set.
Moulded gelatin in pea coats, the team of us.

(It is dusk as I write this.)
The neighbour kids head out for a picnic, banging lids.

Know I found this comforting: that style
is enough, if you love the world enough.

Coveters with rhythm sections
waltz to Christie Pits.

Elegy for the Outdoor Coliseum

For her coiled public: the mass weddings and tattoos,
and the parades that ended in the infield.
For the masked accountants painted blue. For expansion teams.

For the naked men and women who set out like houseflies,
all hair and heightened instincts, to gamble with disclaimers
of paid-duty cops. Who were tackled and were never seen again.

For the time we watched *Crusher* beat
The Last Stand of the Working Class by half a car's length,
and the announcer warned us to Stay Away from Soccer.

For fan conventions. For the couples who fucked
in the bathroom stalls of fan conventions
and crawled out marked with one another's makeup.

For the dancing reverends with their wives, the sponsors
with their naming rights, the dot-com long dead but its logo still
stickered to the balustrade. Tagged like a bested tyrant's face.

For hybridity, the dream of a renewable surface.
For the FieldTurf that burnt at any friction,
or peeled itself off you like a wetsuit underfoot.

For the day they sold the team so we kidnapped the owner,
tied him to the mound for a common prosecution.
For the picture in the paper where he's forced to wear a hat.

For the contest last year where you had to write an essay,
and the winner's team would get her dormant lighting for a night,
the city's parked snowplows rolled away to let them play.

And a child ballerina wrote the chosen essay.
And even though it rained, she took the stage in centre field,
her troupemates tripping up the stairs in stocking feet.

For the mothers spread on blankets, drinking wine.
And in the pause before Brahms's first concerto, for those girls
like a music box our power grid would fail to support.

Notes and Acknowledgements

"Ali Kills Liston": Lewiston, ME, 1965. ∞ "Babushka Lady to Umbrella Man": Dallas, TX, 1963. ∞ "What Humans Like": Emily Howell is the creation of Prof. David Cope et al. ∞ "To the Inhabitants of Tiny Houses from the Internet": Adam Ellis, "13 Truly Adorable Houses You Can Buy for Less than a Year of College," *Buzzfeed*, June 25, 2014. ∞ "John Darnielle as Frank Oz in the Unfilmed Henson Biopic": Italicized passage is from "This Year" by The Mountain Goats (John Darnielle) from *The Sunset Tree* (4AD, 2005). ∞ "A Linda Taylor": Last line paraphrased from Jay-Z, "Otis" (w/ Kanye West) from *Watch the Throne* (Roc-a-Fella/Def Jam, 2011). ∞ "Romulus and Remus and Hannah Arendt": "On Violence," collected in *Crises of the Republic*, "The point, as Marx saw it, was that dreams never come true." ∞ "The Former Jugoslavija": The former Hotel Jugoslavija is on Nikola Tesla Boulevard in Belgrade, Serbia, and is awaiting renovations to convert it into a casino. ∞ "The American Century in Brief*": Source is the shortest sentences from each of Stephen E. Lucas and Martin J. Medhurst's *100 Most Significant American Political Speeches of the 20th Century*, presented chronologically and without additions. ∞ "Unisphere at Midnight": Flushing Meadows, New York City. ∞ "The Short Twentieth, the Long Nineteenth": The "long nineteenth century" (1789–1914) and the "short twentieth century" (1914–1991) are terms from Hobsbawm's *The Age of Revolution* and *The Age of Extremes*, respectively. ∞ "Golf Pro, Monobloc, *A Theory of the Firm*": Title allusion from Michael Jensen's *A Theory of the Firm: Governance, Residual Claims, and Organizational Form* (Harvard University Press, 2003). ∞ "Doomer Meet-Up, University of Toronto": Dan Carlin anecdote is from *Hardcore History* series "The Wrath of the Khans." ∞ "Love Poem after *Industrial Society and Its Future*": Title allusion is Theodore Kaczynski, Special Report Op-Ed, *The New York Times*, September 19, 1995. ∞ "I Will Find You in the Bank Run": Thessaloniki, 2011. ∞ "Alpha Proportionality Dinner": Title inspired by the *Alpha* song cycle by The Mountain Goats

(John Darnielle). ∞ "They Will Take My Island": Title allusion from Arshile Gorky's 1941 painting and the blog of the same name by Paul Vermeersch. ∞ "As an Extra for a Film Shoot at the Quality Cafe": Supercuts are available online showing many of the film and TV scenes shot at the Quality Cafe, 1236 West 7th St., Los Angeles, CA. ∞ "On the Ideology of Trolls": Title inspired by a passage in Ta-Nehisi Coates, "The Good, Racist People," *The New York Times,* March 6, 2013. ∞ "Mark Coleman's Daughters Are Turning Out Okay": Pride 32, Thomas & Mack Center, Las Vegas, NV, October 21, 2006.

Poems have previously appeared in *Arc, Event, Hazlitt, New Poetry, Prairie Fire, Riddle Fence, They Will Take My Island, This, Villamere,* and *The Windsor Review,* as well as the anthologies *Best Canadian Poetry in English* 2012 (Tightrope), *Best Canadian Poetry in English* 2013 (Tightrope), *I Found It At the Movies* (Guernica, 2014), and the chapbook *Vox Populism* (The Emergency Response Unit, 2011).

Thank you to the friends and family who served as early readers for these poems. Thank you to my editor, Kevin Connolly, and to the publishing team at McClelland & Stewart. And thank you to the Canada Council for the Arts, the Ontario Arts Council, and the Writers' Trust of Canada for the financial support of my work and the work of many others.

Thank you to Alexis. Thank you to Oliver.

A NOTE ON THE TYPE

The body of *Don't Be Interesting* has been set in Fairfield, a typeface originally designed by Rudolph Ruzicka for the Linotype Corporation in the 1940s. The face references modern versions of such classic text faces as Bodoni and Didot, and, like its influencial forerunners, Fairfield is at its best when used in book-length text settings.